STONES OF REMEMBRANCE

A MEMORY RESCUE RESOURCE

STONES

OF

REMEMBRANCE

Healing Scriptures for Your
Mind, Body, and Soul

DANIEL G. AMEN, MD

TYNDALE
MOMENTUM™

The nonfiction imprint of
Tyndale House Publishers, Inc.

Visit Tyndale online at www.tyndale.com.

Visit Tyndale Momentum online at www.tyndalemomentum.com.

TYNDALE, Tyndale Momentum, and Tyndale's quill logo are registered trademarks of Tyndale House Publishers, Inc. The Tyndale Momentum logo is a trademark of Tyndale House Publishers, Inc. Tyndale Momentum is the nonfiction imprint of Tyndale House Publishers, Inc., Carol Stream, Illinois.

Stones of Remembrance: Healing Scriptures for Your Mind, Body, and Soul

Designed by Dean H. Renninger

Published in association with the literary agency of WordServe Literary Group, www.wordserveliterary.com.

For information about special discounts for bulk purchases, please contact Tyndale House Publishers at csresponse@tyndale.com, or call 1-800-323-9400.

ISBN 978-1-4964-2667-3

Printed in the United States of America

23   22   21   20   19   18   17
7   6   5   4   3   2   1

Always remember these things after I am gone.

2 PETER 1:15

Contents

Foreword

by Stephen Arterburn, MEd

Dr. Daniel Amen is a champion for the brain. Through his research, insights, and persistence, he helps us value the most incredible lump of mass on the planet and then nurture, develop, protect, and provide for it. Dr. Amen's mission is to show us how to ensure that our brains function at peak performance for as long as possible. And those hundreds of thousands of us who now call ourselves Brain Warriors are fighting for the health, longevity, and effectiveness of our minds, knowing how much they affect every other aspect of our lives.

I first heard of Dr. Amen many years ago when I watched his PBS specials and read his book *Change Your Brain, Change Your Life*. Not long ago, I took the time to see him so he could help me identify what type of attention deficit disorder I had. Instead, he and his team discovered that I had a traumatic brain injury that needed immediate treatment. If it wasn't addressed, I could most likely expect dysfunction and Alzheimer's disease or dementia in my near future. So I became a warrior alongside Dr. Amen, and the results have been beyond my expectations. Following his team's recommendations has made a remarkable difference. My wife listens to me say things from my heart and tells me I never talked that way before. My memory has become sharper, and difficult concepts have become clearer. I will be a grateful Brain Warrior to the end.

Something was missing, however, from all I was doing to work my brain as an athlete works to build muscle. All the brain games and exercises were centered on information and activities I did not care much about. I wanted something different that would help me grow spiritually while I strengthened my brain's ability to function well. *Stones of Remembrance* is exactly what I was looking for.

Since I received my advance copy, I have been able to work my brain while growing spiritually stronger from the power found in knowing God's Word deeply and richly. Every verse studied, memorized, and meditated upon helps me know more, appreciate the depth and width of God's love for me, and strengthen my connection with God. And I'm gaining these spiritual benefits while making the organ that processes all of these verses even stronger.

Using Scripture to further Dr. Amen's work in healing brains is brilliant. It is wisdom upon wisdom when his knowledge is combined with the truth found in the Bible. If you use this enlightening and empowering tool, I believe you will experience both a stronger faith and greater brain power.

I am so glad Dr. Amen didn't develop *Stones of Remembrance* twenty years from now. We can all use it today and experience its benefits for the rest of our lives. I hope that you enjoy this great work as much as I am enjoying it and that it blesses your life as it has blessed mine.

PS My favorite feature is part 3, which includes twelve verses all Christians need to memorize. Don't wait until the end of the book to read them. My suggestion is to start memorizing them from the start.

Introduction

Remember the days of long ago;
think about the generations past.

DEUTERONOMY 32:7

Memory enables us to bring the joys, dreams, and lessons of yesterday into today. As we recall God's faithfulness, we remain centered and growing, and we move forward with a sense of purpose. Memory allows us to keep our loved ones close, even when they are far away. It assures us that our personal history and experiences matter—that we have something valuable to teach the generations to come.

This is the way God designed our minds to work—to *remember*. It's been that way from the very beginning.

In the Old Testament, after the Israelites crossed the Jordan River and entered into the Promised Land, God gave this command to Joshua: "Take twelve stones

. . . and lay them down in the place where you lodge tonight" (Joshua 4:3, ESV). Joshua delegated this task to one leader from each of Israel's twelve tribes and then explained the rocks' significance:

> When your children ask in time to come, "What do those stones mean to you?" then you shall tell them that the waters of the Jordan were cut off before the ark of the covenant of the LORD. . . . So these stones shall be to the people of Israel a *memorial* forever.
>
> JOSHUA 4:6-7, ESV, EMPHASIS ADDED

These twelve stones were God's way of creating a visual reminder of his covenant with the Israelites—a symbol that would stand for generations to come to show that his protection and provision should never be forgotten.

We witness a similar ritual in the New Testament when Jesus breaks bread with his disciples at the Last Supper and says, "This is my body, which is given for you. Do this in *remembrance* of me" (Luke 22:19, emphasis added). To this day, the act of Communion serves as a tangible reminder of Christ's love and sacrifice.

All throughout the Bible, we are encouraged—and even commanded—to remember.

Remember to observe the Sabbath day by keeping it holy.

EXODUS 20:8

Remember and obey all the commands of the LORD instead of following your own desires.

NUMBERS 15:39

Remember the wonders he has performed.

1 CHRONICLES 16:12

Remember the words of the Lord Jesus: "It is more blessed to give than to receive."

ACTS 20:35

Remember, therefore, what you have received and heard; hold it fast, and repent.

REVELATION 3:3, NIV

Remember the things I have done in the past.
    For I alone am God!
    I am God, and there is none like me.

ISAIAH 46:9

Of course, there is a reason the Bible calls us to remember time and again.

Knowing God's promises and obeying his commands are essential to a healthy spiritual life. If you think about it, the Scriptures are a road map for how we are to communicate with God and each other. They direct us in how we are supposed to live. If we stray from his Word—if we forget his promises—then just like a driver without GPS, we will get lost. Meditating on God's Word helps us stay the course—*and* it brings us closer to him.

But it's not just our spiritual well-being that benefits from remembering. Participating in regular spiritual practices such as Scripture meditation, memorization, and prayer also contributes to a healthier mind and body by reducing stress, increasing brain capacity, and even guarding against memory loss.

How? Think of your brain as a muscle. The more you stretch it, the stronger it becomes. The stronger your brain becomes, the stronger your memory becomes. And the stronger your memory becomes, the stronger *you* become. When your brain works right, *you* work right in every area of your life—physically, emotionally, and spiritually. I address the physical and emotional impact of brain health on memory in greater depth in my book *Memory Rescue*. Here, I want to focus on the spiritual impact.

Inside this book are hundreds of carefully selected Scripture passages, just waiting to be read and committed to memory. As you meditate on these verses, not only will you be exercising your brain and strengthening your memory, you also will be gaining a better understanding of how to live a happy, healthy, God-centered life.

If you've struggled with memorization in the past, don't panic. This book is going to help you strengthen an area that *needs* strengthening. And that's a good thing!

To make things a little easier, the book is broken into three parts—each specifically designed to make the memorization process more meaningful and intuitive for you.

Part 1 focuses on the Twelve Spiritual Disciplines for Improving Your Memory. These twelve disciplines are not just the building blocks of a vibrant Christian life, but the foundations of a healthy brain and strong memory as well. The more you can incorporate these disciplines into your daily life, the better you'll think, feel, grow, connect with others, and, yes, remember. To help you recall these twelve keys to healthy living and a strong memory, I have organized them according to the mnemonic device **REMEMBRANCES**.

Rest
Exercise
Meditation and Prayer
Eating Healthy
Meaningful Work
Bonding with Others
Relaxation
Absolution
New Learning
Concentration
Enjoyment
Socialization

I will address the biblical and biological significance of each discipline as we go, but if you're anxious to get started, you can begin by committing the acronym to memory!

In part 2, the Scriptures have been organized by theme. You'll find these verses particularly helpful when you are in need of quick biblical advice, support, or inspiration. After all, during times of anxiety, doubt, joy, or despair, there is no better place to turn than the

Bible—and having these passages committed to memory is even better.

Finally, part 3 highlights the twelve verses every Christian should know. If you're new to Scripture memorization, you may want to start here. These verses capture the very essence of the Christian faith and are wonderful promises to remember in daily life. They are also a great starting place for sharing your faith with others.

If memorization is new for you, start small—just five minutes a day. Begin by reviewing verses you're already familiar with. Then memorize one verse, or even part of a verse, at a time. You'll be surprised by how much you already know. And when you have trouble, don't get discouraged. It may be hard at first, but it's worth it!

Next to your salvation, your memory may be the most incredible gift you've been given. Take care of it. Challenge it. Strengthen it. Most of all, treasure it. God does.

And so should you.

Daniel G. Amen, MD

PART 1

THE TWELVE SPIRITUAL DISCIPLINES FOR IMPROVING YOUR MEMORY

Thank you for making me so wonderfully complex! Your workmanship is marvelous—how well I know it.

PSALM 139:14

1

REST

On the seventh day God had finished his work of creation,
so he rested from all his work.

GENESIS 2:2

It's not a coincidence that so much emphasis is placed on rest in the Bible. God designed our bodies to restore and recharge themselves through sleep. Even he rested on the seventh day (Genesis 2:2). This simple act was important at the dawn of Creation, and it's still important now. When we sleep, our brains actually "clean" themselves. They hit the reset button and ready themselves for another day. Anytime we get fewer than seven hours of sleep, we lessen our capacity to think clearly. Simply put, when our brains don't get enough rest, they start making mistakes. If you want to keep your brain healthy and happy, make sure to get plenty of sleep.

Come to me, all of you who are weary and carry heavy burdens, and I will give you rest.

MATTHEW 11:28

The LORD replied, "I will personally go with you, Moses, and I will give you rest— everything will be fine for you."

EXODUS 33:14

Take my yoke upon you. Let me teach you, because I am humble and gentle at heart, and you will find rest for your souls.

MATTHEW 11:29

You have six days each week for your ordinary work, but on the seventh day you must stop working, even during the seasons of plowing and harvest.

EXODUS 34:21

Be still, and know that I am God!

PSALM 46:10

I have given rest to the weary and joy to the sorrowing.

JEREMIAH 31:25

Youths will become weak and tired,
     and young men will fall in exhaustion.
But those who trust in the LORD will find new
          strength.
     They will soar high on wings like eagles.
They will run and not grow weary.
     They will walk and not faint.

ISAIAH 40:30-31

Remember to observe the Sabbath day by keeping it holy.

EXODUS 20:8

In peace I will lie down and sleep,
     for you alone, O LORD, will keep me safe.

PSALM 4:8

I lay down and slept,
    yet I woke up in safety,
    for the LORD was watching over me.

PSALM 3:5

Only in returning to me
    and resting in me will you be saved.
In quietness and confidence is your strength.

ISAIAH 30:15

EXERCISE

Don't you realize that your body is the temple of the Holy
Spirit, who lives in you and was given to you by God?

I CORINTHIANS 6:19

As the apostle Paul states in 1 Corinthians, your body is a temple of the Holy Spirit. This temple houses your brain—the complex and powerful command and control center that runs your life. That's why it is so important to take good care of your mind, and exercising regularly is a great way to start. Not only does exercise keep you fit, it increases blood flow to your brain, which helps you focus, think, learn, and remember.

God bought you with a high price. So you
must honor God with your body.

I CORINTHIANS 6:20

Dear friend, I hope all is well with you and that you are as healthy in body as you are strong in spirit.

3 JOHN 1:2

I discipline my body like an athlete, training it to do what it should. Otherwise, I fear that after preaching to others I myself might be disqualified.

1 CORINTHIANS 9:27

The Sovereign LORD is my strength!
He makes me as surefooted as a
deer,
able to tread upon the heights.

HABAKKUK 3:19

The wise are mightier than the strong,
   and those with knowledge grow stronger and
      stronger.

PROVERBS 24:5

I can do everything through Christ, who gives
me strength.

PHILIPPIANS 4:13

I have fought the good fight, I have finished the
race, and I have remained faithful.

2 TIMOTHY 4:7

Dear brothers and sisters, I plead with you to
give your bodies to God because of all he has
done for you. Let them be a living and holy
sacrifice—the kind he will find acceptable. This
is truly the way to worship him.

ROMANS 12:1

Don't be impressed with your own wisdom.
    Instead, fear the LORD and turn away from evil.
Then you will have healing for your body
    and strength for your bones.

PROVERBS 3:7-8

"I will give you back your health
   and heal your wounds," says the LORD.
"For you are called an outcast—
   'Jerusalem for whom no one cares.'"

JEREMIAH 30:17

All athletes are disciplined in their training.
They do it to win a prize that will fade away,
but we do it for an eternal prize. So I run with
purpose in every step.

I CORINTHIANS 9:25-26

MEDITATION AND PRAYER

Pray without ceasing.

I THESSALONIANS 5:17, ESV

Not only are meditation and prayer vital to a healthy spiritual life, they are also wonderful stress-management tools and powerful prefrontal cortex boosters. In fact, research has shown that people who pray and meditate regularly have better focus and executive function than those who don't. They also have better judgment and impulse control, which enable them to make more thoughtful and moral decisions. As you meditate on the following verses, aim to open yourself up fully to the calming and restorative presence of God.

If you remain in me and my words remain in you, you may ask for anything you want, and it will be granted!

JOHN 15:7

The LORD hears his people when they call to him for help. He rescues them from all their troubles.

PSALM 34:17

I tell you, you can pray for anything, and if you believe that you've received it, it will be yours.

MARK 11:24

Ask me and I will tell you remarkable secrets you do not know about things to come.

JEREMIAH 33:3

Pray like this:

Our Father in heaven,
    may your name be kept holy.
May your Kingdom come soon.
May your will be done on earth,
    as it is in heaven.
Give us today the food we need,
and forgive us our sins,
    as we have forgiven those who sin against us.
And don't let us yield to temptation,
    but rescue us from the evil one.

MATTHEW 6:9-13

To you who are willing to listen, I say, love your enemies! Do good to those who hate you. Bless those who curse you. Pray for those who hurt you.

LUKE 6:27-28

The earnest prayer of a righteous person has great power and produces wonderful results.

JAMES 5:16

If two of you agree here on earth concerning anything you ask, my Father in heaven will do it for you. For where two or three gather together as my followers, I am there among them.

MATTHEW 18:19-20

In those days when you pray, I will listen.

JEREMIAH 29:12

You can pray for anything, and if you have faith, you will receive it.

MATTHEW 21:22

I tell you, keep on asking, and you will receive what you ask for. Keep on seeking, and you will find. Keep on knocking, and the door will be opened to you. For everyone who asks, receives. Everyone who seeks, finds. And to everyone who knocks, the door will be opened.

LUKE 11:9-10

EATING HEALTHY

Whether you eat or drink, or whatever you do,
do it all for the glory of God.

I CORINTHIANS 10:31

You've most likely heard the phrase "You are what you eat." In many respects, this is true. Your brain is the most energy-hungry organ in your body. In fact, 20 to 30 percent of the calories you consume go directly to your brain. If you eat a fast-food diet, you can expect to have a fast-food mind that is less capable of thinking clearly. On the other hand, supplying your body with fruits, vegetables, and lean proteins boosts your brain's functionality. First Corinthians 10:31 says that eating and drinking should be done for the glory of God. To keep your memory and spiritual life healthy, it is important to focus on eating brain-healthy food.

God said, "Look! I have given you every seed-bearing plant throughout the earth and all the fruit trees for your food."

GENESIS 1:29

I discipline my body and keep it under control.

I CORINTHIANS 9:27, ESV

Since everything God created is good, we should not reject any of it but receive it with thanks. For we know it is made acceptable by the word of God and prayer.

1 TIMOTHY 4:4-5

Jesus replied, "I am the bread of life. Whoever comes to me will never be hungry again. Whoever believes in me will never be thirsty."

JOHN 6:35

People do not live by bread alone; rather, we live by every word that comes from the mouth of the Lord.

DEUTERONOMY 8:3

If you will only obey me,
   you will have plenty to eat.

ISAIAH 1:19

Don't be so concerned about perishable things like food. Spend your energy seeking the eternal life that the Son of Man can give you. For God the Father has given me the seal of his approval.

JOHN 6:27

It's not good to eat too much honey,
   and it's not good to seek honors for yourself.

PROVERBS 25:27

I have not departed from his commands,
   but have treasured his words more than daily
      food.

JOB 23:12

God blesses those who hunger and thirst
            for justice,
      for they will be satisfied.

MATTHEW 5:6

How sweet your words taste to me;
      they are sweeter than honey.

PSALM 119:103

MEANINGFUL WORK

Work willingly at whatever you do, as though you were
working for the Lord rather than for people. Remember
that the Lord will give you an inheritance as your reward,
and that the Master you are serving is Christ.

COLOSSIANS 3:23-24

Though we may complain about our jobs from time to time, the truth is, work is a good thing, especially when that work is meaningful. It gives us passion and a sense of purpose. When we have motivation for our work that goes beyond just making money, that passion lights up our limbic systems, which play a key role in our brains' response to emotional stimulation. From a spiritual standpoint, when we commit ourselves to working wholeheartedly for the Lord, we become godlier in return. Our brains have actually been wired that way. Let this be an encouragement to do meaningful work, knowing God will reward our efforts!

May the Lord our God show us his approval
and make our efforts successful.

PSALM 90:17

The LORD God placed the man in the Garden
of Eden to tend and watch over it.

GENESIS 2:15

**Be strong and immovable.
Always work enthusiastically
for the Lord, for you know that
nothing you do for the Lord is
ever useless.**

1 CORINTHIANS 15:58

Let your good deeds shine out for all to see, so
that everyone will praise your heavenly Father.

MATTHEW 5:16

I have been a constant example of how you can help those in need by working hard. You should remember the words of the Lord Jesus: "It is more blessed to give than to receive."

ACTS 20:35

I brought glory to you here on earth by completing the work you gave me to do.

JOHN 17:4

Get up, for it is your duty to tell us how to proceed in setting things straight. We are behind you, so be strong and take action.

EZRA 10:4

God is not unjust. He will not forget how hard you have worked for him and how you have shown your love to him by caring for other believers.

HEBREWS 6:10

You will enjoy the fruit of your labor.
How joyful and prosperous you will be!

PSALM 128:2

God has given each of you a gift from his great variety of spiritual gifts. Use them well to serve one another.

1 PETER 4:10

I . . . found great pleasure in hard work, a reward for all my labors.

ECCLESIASTES 2:10

BONDING WITH OTHERS

Let all that you do be done in love.

1 CORINTHIANS 16:14, ESV

The simple act of loving others is one of the best—and most enjoyable—ways you can care for your brain. In fact, new research has shown that developing feelings of goodwill, kindness, and warmth toward others not only increases positive emotions, it can actually combat depression, decrease pain and negative feelings, and help eliminate migraines. In other words, love brings healing. Follow the apostle Paul's admonition: "Let all that you do be done in love."

Love is patient and kind; love does not envy or boast; it is not arrogant or rude. It does not insist on its own way; it is not irritable or resentful; it does not rejoice at wrongdoing, but rejoices with the truth. Love bears all things, believes all things, hopes all things, endures all things. Love never ends.

1 CORINTHIANS 13:4-8, ESV

Let us continue to love one another, for love comes from God. Anyone who loves is a child of God and knows God.

1 JOHN 4:7

You were cleansed from your sins when you obeyed the truth, so now you must show sincere love to each other as brothers and sisters. Love each other deeply with all your heart.

1 PETER 1:22

Anyone who does not love does not know God, for God is love.

1 JOHN 4:8

You must love the LORD your God with all your
heart, all your soul, all your mind, and all your
strength.

MARK 12:30

I am giving you a new commandment: Love
each other. Just as I have loved you, you should
love each other. Your love for one another will
prove to the world that you are my disciples.

JOHN 13:34-35

There is no greater love than to lay down one's
life for one's friends.

JOHN 15:13

This is how God loved the world: He gave
his one and only Son, so that everyone who
believes in him will not perish but have
eternal life.

JOHN 3:16

We love each other because he loved us first.

1 JOHN 4:19

Such love has no fear, because perfect love expels all fear. If we are afraid, it is for fear of punishment, and this shows that we have not fully experienced his perfect love.

1 JOHN 4:18

Love your enemies! Do good to them. Lend to them without expecting to be repaid. Then your reward from heaven will be very great, and you will truly be acting as children of the Most High, for he is kind to those who are unthankful and wicked.

LUKE 6:35

RELAXATION

*Come to me, all of you who are weary and carry heavy
burdens, and I will give you rest. Take my yoke upon you.
Let me teach you, because I am humble and gentle at heart,
and you will find rest for your souls.*

MATTHEW 11:28-29

At one point or another, all of us experience stress. Though
a little stress can be a good thing—it keeps us moving and
working—too much can have a negative effect on our
brains. In fact, too much stress can destroy brain cells,
leading us to make bad decisions, lash out at others, and
forget things. In Matthew 11:28-29, Jesus encourages us
to let go of our burdens and rest in him. There is no better way to do that than to spend time praying and quietly
meditating on his Word.

I am leaving you with a gift—peace of mind and heart. And the peace I give is a gift the world cannot give. So don't be troubled or afraid.

JOHN 14:27

Give your burdens to the LORD,
    and he will take care of you.
    He will not permit the godly to slip and fall.

PSALM 55:22

In my distress I prayed to the LORD,
    and the LORD answered me and set me free.
The LORD is for me, so I will have no fear.
    What can mere people do to me?

PSALM 118:5-6

Jesus said, "Let's go off by ourselves to a quiet place and rest awhile."

MARK 6:31

We know that God causes everything to work together for the good of those who love God and are called according to his purpose.

ROMANS 8:28

Don't worry about tomorrow, for tomorrow will bring its own worries. Today's trouble is enough for today.

MATTHEW 6:34

This is my command—be strong and courageous! Do not be afraid or discouraged. For the LORD your God is with you wherever you go.

JOSHUA 1:9

The LORD is my shepherd;
    I have all that I need.
He lets me rest in green meadows;
    he leads me beside peaceful streams.
He renews my strength.

PSALM 23:1-3

Can all your worries add a single moment to your life?

LUKE 12:25

God has not given us a spirit of fear and timidity, but of power, love, and self-discipline.

2 TIMOTHY 1:7

There is nothing better than to be happy and enjoy ourselves as long as we can. And people should eat and drink and enjoy the fruits of their labor, for these are gifts from God.

ECCLESIASTES 3:12-13

ABSOLUTION

Hatred stirs up quarrels, but love makes up for all offenses.

PROVERBS 10:12

Nothing wreaks havoc on your body and soul quite like bitterness and hatred. When you hold on to anger and resentment, the cells in your body are put into a tense state, which damages your immune system and impairs your ability to think and remember things clearly. However, much like love, forgiveness brings healing. When you forgive, you let go of negativity and pain, restoring your body and mind to a healthy state. As you meditate on the following verses, think of someone you are struggling to forgive, and ask God to help you let go of your anger. You will be amazed by how healing it is to forgive.

When you are praying, first forgive anyone
you are holding a grudge against, so that your
Father in heaven will forgive your sins, too.

MARK 11:25

Confess your sins to each other
and pray for each other so that
you may be healed. The earnest
prayer of a righteous person
has great power and produces
wonderful results.

JAMES 5:16

Be kind to each other, tenderhearted, forgiving
one another, just as God through Christ has
forgiven you.

EPHESIANS 4:32

If you refuse to forgive others, your Father will not forgive your sins.

MATTHEW 6:15

If we confess our sins to him, he is faithful and just to forgive us our sins and to cleanse us from all wickedness.

I JOHN 1:9

Peter came to him and asked, "Lord, how often should I forgive someone who sins against me? Seven times?"

"No, not seven times," Jesus replied, "but seventy times seven!"

MATTHEW 18:21-22

Love your enemies! Do good to those who hate you.

LUKE 6:27

Do not judge others, and you will not be judged. Do not condemn others, or it will all come back against you. Forgive others, and you will be forgiven.

LUKE 6:37

Make allowance for each other's faults, and
forgive anyone who offends you. Remember,
the Lord forgave you, so you must forgive
others.

COLOSSIANS 3:13

If your enemies are hungry, give them food to eat.
  If they are thirsty, give them water to drink.

PROVERBS 25:21

The wages of sin is death, but the free gift of
God is eternal life through Christ Jesus our Lord.

ROMANS 6:23

NEW LEARNING

Intelligent people are always ready to learn.
Their ears are open for knowledge.

PROVERBS 18:15

You are never too old to learn. Unfortunately, many people become less active with age, causing their blood flow to drop and increasing their susceptibility to memory problems, brain fog, and depression. In other words, when you stop learning, your brain starts dying. However, there is good news. Research shows that people who keep their minds active tend to live longer and are less likely to fall victim to diseases like Alzheimer's and dementia. So keep learning new things. Study God's Word. Commit new verses to memory. Not only will this time spent in the Bible draw you closer to the Creator, it will keep your mind healthy, vibrant, and alert for years to come.

Let the wise listen to these proverbs and become
even wiser.
Let those with understanding receive guidance.

PROVERBS 1:5

Instruct the wise,
and they will be even wiser.
Teach the righteous,
and they will learn even more.

PROVERBS 9:9

Get wisdom; develop good
judgment.
Don't forget my words or turn
away from them.

PROVERBS 4:5

Fear of the LORD is the foundation of true
knowledge,
but fools despise wisdom and discipline.

PROVERBS 1:7

The wisdom from above is first pure, then peaceable, gentle, open to reason, full of mercy and good fruits, impartial and sincere.

JAMES 3:17, ESV

Show me the right path, O LORD;
 point out the road for me to follow.
Lead me by your truth and teach me,
 for you are the God who saves me.
 All day long I put my hope in you.

PSALM 25:4-5

Such things were written in the Scriptures long ago to teach us. And the Scriptures give us hope and encouragement as we wait patiently for God's promises to be fulfilled.

ROMANS 15:4

Jesus told him, "I am the way, the truth, and the life. No one can come to the Father except through me."

JOHN 14:6

Keep putting into practice all you learned and received from me—everything you heard from me and saw me doing. Then the God of peace will be with you.

PHILIPPIANS 4:9

The LORD says, "I will guide you along the best
      pathway for your life.
  I will advise you and watch over you."

PSALM 32:8

If you need wisdom, ask our generous God, and he will give it to you. He will not rebuke you for asking.

JAMES 1:5

CONCENTRATION

*Look straight ahead, and fix your eyes on
what lies before you.*

PROVERBS 4:25

It's easy to become distracted, to let your mind wander away
from the good and focus on the bad. But doing so is harmful
to your mental well-being. The more you learn to block out
negative thoughts and concentrate on what is truly important—like your loved ones and your relationship with God—
the deeper your bond will be with both, and the healthier
your brain will be. As you meditate on the following verses,
keep your mind focused on the positive, and let your body
and soul reap the benefits of God's healing words.

Think about the things of heaven, not the things of earth.

COLOSSIANS 3:2

Seek the Kingdom of God above all else, and live righteously, and he will give you everything you need.

MATTHEW 6:33

Fix your thoughts on what is true, and honorable, and right, and pure, and lovely, and admirable. Think about things that are excellent and worthy of praise.

PHILIPPIANS 4:8

Commit your actions to the LORD, and your plans will succeed.

PROVERBS 16:3

Don't copy the behavior and customs of this world, but let God transform you into a new person by changing the way you think. Then you will learn to know God's will for you, which is good and pleasing and perfect.

ROMANS 12:2

The one who endures to the end will be saved.

MATTHEW 24:13

Work hard so you can present yourself to God and receive his approval. Be a good worker, one who does not need to be ashamed and who correctly explains the word of truth.

2 TIMOTHY 2:15

Let us hold tightly without wavering to the hope we affirm, for God can be trusted to keep his promise.

HEBREWS 10:23

Your word is a lamp to guide my feet
    and a light for my path.

PSALM 119:105

Joyful are those who obey his laws
  and search for him with all their hearts.

PSALM 119:2

We must listen very carefully to the truth we
have heard, or we may drift away from it.

HEBREWS 2:1

ENJOYMENT

Fix your thoughts on what is true, and honorable, and right, and pure, and lovely, and admirable.

PHILIPPIANS 4:8

Where you direct your attention determines how you feel. If you are prone to thinking about negative situations—times when you felt slighted or belittled—naturally, you will feel depressed. And depression is one of the risk factors for Alzheimer's disease. However, when you think about good things—the people you love or the beauty of nature—you will feel happy. And a happy brain is a healthy brain. Start every day with the phrase "Today is going to be a great day," and keep your thoughts fixed on what is true, honorable, right, pure, and lovely. Your brain will thank you.

When troubles of any kind come your way, consider it an opportunity for great joy.

JAMES 1:2

The Holy Spirit produces this kind of fruit in our lives: love, joy, peace, patience, kindness, goodness, faithfulness, gentleness, and self-control.

GALATIANS 5:22-23

Always be full of joy in the Lord. I say it again—rejoice!

PHILIPPIANS 4:4

I pray that God, the source of hope, will fill you completely with joy and peace because you trust in him. Then you will overflow with confident hope through the power of the Holy Spirit.

ROMANS 15:13

Ask, using my name, and you will receive, and
you will have abundant joy.

JOHN 16:24

You love him even though you have never
seen him. Though you do not see him now,
you trust him; and you rejoice with a glorious,
inexpressible joy.

1 PETER 1:8

A cheerful heart is good medicine,
but a broken spirit saps a person's strength.

PROVERBS 17:22

Always be joyful.

1 THESSALONIANS 5:16

This is the day the LORD has made.
We will rejoice and be glad in it.

PSALM 118:24

In him our hearts rejoice,
for we trust in his holy name.

PSALM 33:21

The LORD is my strength and shield.
    I trust him with all my heart.
He helps me, and my heart is filled with joy.
    I burst out in songs of thanksgiving.

PSALM 28:7

SOCIALIZATION

It is not good for the man to be alone.

GENESIS 2:18

When God created humans, he knew it was not good for us to be alone. He designed us to be a social species. We need other people in our lives to thrive emotionally and spiritually. Without friends and family to interact with, our minds begin to decay. In fact, studies have shown that feeling lonely is a risk factor for Alzheimer's. If you're looking for new ways to build community, try getting involved with your church, taking a class, forming friendships at work, sharing a meal with your neighbors, and staying connected with old friends. Not only is having community good for your soul, it's good for your brain as well!

Encourage each other and build each other up, just as you are already doing.

1 THESSALONIANS 5:11

Most important of all, continue to show deep love for each other, for love covers a multitude of sins.

1 PETER 4:8

A person standing alone can be attacked and defeated, but two can stand back-to-back and conquer. Three are even better, for a triple-braided cord is not easily broken.

ECCLESIASTES 4:12

As iron sharpens iron, so a friend sharpens a friend.

PROVERBS 27:17

A friend is always loyal,
and a brother is born to help in time of need.

PROVERBS 17:17

Let us think of ways to motivate one another to acts of love and good works. And let us not neglect our meeting together, as some people do, but encourage one another, especially now that the day of his return is drawing near.

HEBREWS 10:24-25

Love your neighbor as yourself.

MATTHEW 22:39

All of you together are Christ's body, and each of you is a part of it.

1 CORINTHIANS 12:27

We proclaim to you what we ourselves have actually seen and heard so that you may have fellowship with us. And our fellowship is with the Father and with his Son, Jesus Christ.

1 JOHN 1:3

All of you should be of one mind. Sympathize with each other. Love each other as brothers and sisters. Be tenderhearted, and keep a humble attitude.

1 PETER 3:8

When we get together, I want to encourage you in your faith, but I also want to be encouraged by yours.

ROMANS 1:12

PART 2

THE
TWELVE VERSES
TO REMEMBER
WHEN...

The LORD grants wisdom! From his mouth
come knowledge and understanding.

PROVERBS 2:6

YOU ARE ANXIOUS

Don't worry about anything; instead, pray about everything. Tell God what you need, and thank him for all he has done. Then you will experience God's peace, which exceeds anything we can understand. His peace will guard your hearts and minds as you live in Christ Jesus.

PHILIPPIANS 4:6-7

Don't worry about tomorrow, for tomorrow will bring its own worries. Today's trouble is enough for today.

MATTHEW 6:34

Say to those with fearful hearts,
    "Be strong, and do not fear,
for your God is coming to destroy your enemies.
    He is coming to save you."

ISAIAH 35:4

Worry weighs a person down;
  an encouraging word cheers a person up.

PROVERBS 12:25

Humble yourselves under the mighty power
of God, and at the right time he will lift you
up in honor. Give all your worries and cares
to God, for he cares about you.

I PETER 5:6-7

Take my yoke upon you. Let me teach you,
because I am humble and gentle at heart, and
you will find rest for your souls.

MATTHEW 11:29

I know the LORD is always with me.
  I will not be shaken, for he is right beside me.

PSALM 16:8

Can all your worries add a single moment
to your life?

MATTHEW 6:27

I am leaving you with a gift—peace of mind and heart. And the peace I give is a gift the world cannot give. So don't be troubled or afraid.

JOHN 14:27

Don't be afraid, little flock. For it gives your Father great happiness to give you the Kingdom.

LUKE 12:32

The LORD is my helper,
    so I will have no fear.
    What can mere people do to me?

HEBREWS 13:6

Give your burdens to the LORD,
    and he will take care of you.
    He will not permit the godly to slip and fall.

PSALM 55:22

The Twelve Verses to Remember When . . .

YOU ARE GRATEFUL

This is the day the LORD has made.
　　We will rejoice and be glad in it.

PSALM 118:24

Be thankful in all circumstances, for this is God's will for you who belong to Christ Jesus.

1 THESSALONIANS 5:18

Whatever you do or say, do it as a representative of the Lord Jesus, giving thanks through him to God the Father.

COLOSSIANS 3:17

Give thanks to the LORD, for he is good!
　　His faithful love endures forever.

PSALM 136:1

Let us offer through Jesus a continual sacrifice of praise to God, proclaiming our allegiance to his name.

HEBREWS 13:15

The LORD is my strength and shield.
  I trust him with all my heart.
He helps me, and my heart is filled with joy.
  I burst out in songs of thanksgiving.

PSALM 28:7

Whatever is good and perfect is a gift coming down to us from God our Father, who created all the lights in the heavens. He never changes or casts a shifting shadow.

JAMES 1:17

Since we are receiving a Kingdom that is unshakable, let us be thankful and please God by worshiping him with holy fear and awe.

HEBREWS 12:28

Every time I think of you, I give thanks to my God.

PHILIPPIANS 1:3

Give thanks to the LORD and proclaim his
  greatness.
  Let the whole world know what he has done.

1 CHRONICLES 16:8

When troubles of any kind come your way, consider it an opportunity for great joy. For you know that when your faith is tested, your endurance has a chance to grow.

JAMES 1:2-3

I will thank the LORD because he is just;
I will sing praise to the name of the LORD
Most High.

PSALM 7:17

YOU ARE AFRAID

Don't be afraid, for I am with you.

Don't be discouraged, for I am your God.
I will strengthen you and help you.

I will hold you up with my victorious right
hand.

ISAIAH 41:10

God has not given us a spirit of fear and
timidity, but of power, love, and self-discipline.

2 TIMOTHY 1:7

Such love has no fear, because perfect love
expels all fear. If we are afraid, it is for fear of
punishment, and this shows that we have not
fully experienced his perfect love.

1 JOHN 4:18

I prayed to the LORD, and he answered me.

He freed me from all my fears.

PSALM 34:4

Fearing people is a dangerous trap,
   but trusting the LORD means safety.

PROVERBS 29:25

The LORD is my light and my salvation—
   so why should I be afraid?
The LORD is my fortress, protecting me from
      danger,
   so why should I tremble?

PSALM 27:1

I praise God for what he has promised.
   I trust in God, so why should I be afraid?
   What can mere mortals do to me?

PSALM 56:4

This is my command—be strong and
courageous! Do not be afraid or discouraged.
For the LORD your God is with you wherever
you go.

JOSHUA 1:9

You have not received a spirit that makes you
fearful slaves. Instead, you received God's Spirit

when he adopted you as his own children. Now
we call him, "Abba, Father."

ROMANS 8:15

Fear of the LORD is the foundation of true wisdom.
　　All who obey his commandments will grow in
　　　　wisdom.
Praise him forever!

PSALM 111:10

Do not be afraid and do not panic. . . . For the
LORD your God will personally go ahead of
you. He will neither fail you nor abandon you.

DEUTERONOMY 31:6

When I am afraid,
　　I will put my trust in you.

PSALM 56:3

YOU ARE DEPRESSED

He will wipe every tear from their eyes, and there will be no more death or sorrow or crying or pain. All these things are gone forever.

REVELATION 21:4

I have told you all this so that you may have peace in me. Here on earth you will have many trials and sorrows. But take heart, because I have overcome the world.

JOHN 16:33

His anger lasts only a moment,
   but his favor lasts a lifetime!
Weeping may last through the night,
   but joy comes with the morning.

PSALM 30:5

What we suffer now is nothing compared to the glory he will reveal to us later.

ROMANS 8:18

Why am I discouraged?
　Why is my heart so sad?
I will put my hope in God!
　I will praise him again—
　my Savior and my God!

PSALM 42:11

God blesses those who mourn,
　for they will be comforted.

MATTHEW 5:4

Don't let your hearts be troubled. Trust in God,
and trust also in me.

JOHN 14:1

The LORD is close to the brokenhearted;
　he rescues those whose spirits are crushed.

PSALM 34:18

You have turned my mourning into joyful dancing.
　You have taken away my clothes of mourning
　　and clothed me with joy.

PSALM 30:11

In his kindness God called you to share in his eternal glory by means of Christ Jesus. So after you have suffered a little while, he will restore, support, and strengthen you, and he will place you on a firm foundation.

1 PETER 5:10

Those who live in the shelter of the Most High
    will find rest in the shadow of the Almighty.
This I declare about the LORD:
He alone is my refuge, my place of safety;
    he is my God, and I trust him.

PSALM 91:1-2

Do not be afraid or discouraged, for the LORD will personally go ahead of you. He will be with you; he will neither fail you nor abandon you.

DEUTERONOMY 31:8

YOU ARE HAPPY

I will give repeated thanks to the LORD,
    praising him to everyone.

PSALM 109:30

O LORD, I will honor and praise your name,
    for you are my God.
You do such wonderful things!
    You planned them long ago,
    and now you have accomplished them.

ISAIAH 25:1

I can never stop praising you;
    I declare your glory all day long.

PSALM 71:8

I will praise God's name with singing,
    and I will honor him with thanksgiving.

PSALM 69:30

Everything comes from him and exists by his power and is intended for his glory. All glory to him forever! Amen.

ROMANS 11:36

Shout to the LORD, all the earth;
    break out in praise and sing for joy!
Sing your praise to the LORD with the harp,
    with the harp and melodious song,
with trumpets and the sound of the ram's horn.
    Make a joyful symphony before the LORD,
        the King!

PSALM 98:4-6

Whatever is good and perfect is a gift coming down to us from God our Father, who created all the lights in the heavens. He never changes or casts a shifting shadow.

JAMES 1:17

Give thanks to the LORD, for he is good!
    His faithful love endures forever.

PSALM 118:1

Since we are receiving a Kingdom that is unshakable, let us be thankful and please God by worshiping him with holy fear and awe.

HEBREWS 12:28

Sing to the LORD, for he has done wonderful
    things.
    Make known his praise around the world.

ISAIAH 12:5

Give thanks for everything to God the Father in the name of our Lord Jesus Christ.

EPHESIANS 5:20

Great is his faithfulness;
    his mercies begin afresh each morning.

LAMENTATIONS 3:23

The Twelve Verses to Remember When . . .

YOU EXPERIENCE DOUBT

When you ask him, be sure that your faith is in God alone. Do not waver, for a person with divided loyalty is as unsettled as a wave of the sea that is blown and tossed by the wind.

JAMES 1:6

Jesus told them, "I tell you the truth, if you have faith and don't doubt, you can do things like this and much more. You can even say to this mountain, 'May you be lifted up and thrown into the sea,' and it will happen."

MATTHEW 21:21

The blind see, the lame walk, those with leprosy are cured, the deaf hear, the dead are raised to life, and the Good News is being preached to the poor.

MATTHEW 11:5

Don't be afraid, for I am with you.
    Don't be discouraged, for I am your God.

I will strengthen you and help you.
  I will hold you up with my victorious right
    hand.

ISAIAH 41:10

Is anything too hard for the LORD?

GENESIS 18:14

Don't let your hearts be troubled. Trust in God,
and trust also in me.

JOHN 14:1

Faith comes from hearing, that is, hearing the
Good News about Christ.

ROMANS 10:17

I am confident I will see the LORD's goodness
  while I am here in the land of the living.
Wait patiently for the LORD.
  Be brave and courageous.
  Yes, wait patiently for the LORD.

PSALM 27:13-14

Ask me and I will tell you remarkable secrets
you do not know about things to come.

JEREMIAH 33:3

Don't be impressed with your own wisdom.
    Instead, fear the LORD and turn away from evil.
Then you will have healing for your body
    and strength for your bones.

PROVERBS 3:7-8

Faith shows the reality of what we hope for; it is
the evidence of things we cannot see.

HEBREWS 11:1

The word of God will never fail.

LUKE 1:37

YOU ARE LONELY

I will never leave you nor forsake you.

HEBREWS 13:5, ESV

Turn to me and have mercy,
  for I am alone and in deep distress.

PSALM 25:16

Can a mother forget her nursing child?
  Can she feel no love for the child she has borne?
But even if that were possible,
  I would not forget you!
See, I have written your name on the palms of my
    hands.

ISAIAH 49:15-16

No one will be able to stand against you as long
as you live. For I will be with you as I was with
Moses. I will not fail you or abandon you.

JOSHUA 1:5

Even when I walk
    through the darkest valley,
I will not be afraid,
    for you are close beside me.
Your rod and your staff
    protect and comfort me.

PSALM 23:4

Trust in him at all times, O people;
    pour out your heart before him;
    God is a refuge for us.

PSALM 62:8, ESV

No power in the sky above or in the earth
below—indeed, nothing in all creation will ever
be able to separate us from the love of God that
is revealed in Christ Jesus our Lord.

ROMANS 8:39

No, I will not abandon you as orphans—I will
come to you.

JOHN 14:18

Even if my father and mother abandon me,
the LORD will hold me close.

PSALM 27:10

Teach these new disciples to obey all the
commands I have given you. And be sure of
this: I am with you always, even to the end of
the age.

MATTHEW 28:20

If I ride the wings of the morning,
if I dwell by the farthest oceans,
even there your hand will guide me,
and your strength will support me.

PSALM 139:9-10

Father to the fatherless, defender of widows—
this is God, whose dwelling is holy.
God places the lonely in families;
he sets the prisoners free and gives them joy.
But he makes the rebellious live in a sun-scorched
land.

PSALM 68:5-6

YOU ARE SICK

Such a prayer offered in faith will heal the sick, and the Lord will make you well.

JAMES 5:15

Dear friend, I hope all is well with you and that you are as healthy in body as you are strong in spirit.

3 JOHN 1:2

We can rejoice, too, when we run into problems and trials, for we know that they help us develop endurance. And endurance develops strength of character, and character strengthens our confident hope of salvation.

ROMANS 5:3-4

He will wipe every tear from their eyes, and there will be no more death or sorrow or crying or pain. All these things are gone forever.

REVELATION 21:4

Let all that I am praise the LORD;
    may I never forget the good things he does for
      me.
He forgives all my sins
    and heals all my diseases.

PSALM 103:2-3

He gives power to the weak
    and strength to the powerless.
Even youths will become weak and tired,
    and young men will fall in exhaustion.
But those who trust in the LORD will find new
      strength.
    They will soar high on wings like eagles.
They will run and not grow weary.
    They will walk and not faint.

ISAIAH 40:29-31

He personally carried our sins
    in his body on the cross
so that we can be dead to sin
    and live for what is right.
By his wounds
    you are healed.

1 PETER 2:24

A cheerful heart is good medicine,
    but a broken spirit saps a person's strength.

PROVERBS 17:22

Those who live in the shelter of the Most High
    will find rest in the shadow of the Almighty.

PSALM 91:1

I long to visit you so I can bring you some
spiritual gift that will help you grow strong
in the Lord. When we get together, I want to
encourage you in your faith, but I also want to
be encouraged by yours.

ROMANS 1:11-12

Jesus looked at them intently and said,
"Humanly speaking, it is impossible. But not
with God. Everything is possible with God."

MARK 10:27

The Spirit of God, who raised Jesus from the dead,
lives in you. And just as God raised Christ Jesus
from the dead, he will give life to your mortal
bodies by this same Spirit living within you.

ROMANS 8:11

YOU ARE ANGRY

You must all be quick to listen, slow to speak,
and slow to get angry.

JAMES 1:19

Sensible people control their temper;
    they earn respect by overlooking wrongs.

PROVERBS 19:11

Control your temper,
    for anger labels you a fool.

ECCLESIASTES 7:9

A gentle answer deflects anger,
    but harsh words make tempers flare.

PROVERBS 15:1

The LORD is compassionate and merciful,
    slow to get angry and filled with unfailing love.

PSALM 103:8

Love is . . . not irritable, and it keeps no record of being wronged.

1 CORINTHIANS 13:4-5

Stop being angry!
    Turn from your rage!
Do not lose your temper—
    it only leads to harm.

PSALM 37:8

People with understanding control their anger;
    a hot temper shows great foolishness.

PROVERBS 14:29

Human anger does not produce the righteousness God desires.

JAMES 1:20

Get rid of all bitterness, rage, anger, harsh words, and slander, as well as all types of evil behavior.

EPHESIANS 4:31

Fools vent their anger,
    but the wise quietly hold it back.

PROVERBS 29:11

A hot-tempered person starts fights;
    a cool-tempered person stops them.

PROVERBS 15:18

YOU NEED STRENGTH

I can do everything through Christ, who gives me strength.

PHILIPPIANS 4:13

Be on guard. Stand firm in the faith. Be courageous. Be strong.

1 CORINTHIANS 16:13

The LORD your God is going with you! He will fight for you against your enemies, and he will give you victory!

DEUTERONOMY 20:4

The temptations in your life are no different from what others experience. And God is faithful. He will not allow the temptation to be more than you can stand. When you are tempted, he will show you a way out so that you can endure.

1 CORINTHIANS 10:13

Be strong and courageous,
     all you who put your hope in the Lord!

PSALM 31:24

The Lord is my strength and my song;
     he has given me victory.
This is my God, and I will praise him—
     my father's God, and I will exalt him!

EXODUS 15:2

This is what the Sovereign Lord,
     the Holy One of Israel, says:
"Only in returning to me
     and resting in me will you be saved.
In quietness and confidence is your strength."

ISAIAH 30:15

Be strong in the Lord and in his mighty power.

EPHESIANS 6:10

The Lord is for me, so I will have no fear.
     What can mere people do to me?

PSALM 118:6

You must love the LORD your God with all your heart, all your soul, all your mind, and all your strength.

MARK 12:30

My health may fail, and my spirit may grow weak,
    but God remains the strength of my heart;
    he is mine forever.

PSALM 73:26

The joy of the LORD is your strength!

NEHEMIAH 8:10

YOU ARE TIRED

God blesses those who patiently endure testing and temptation. Afterward they will receive the crown of life that God has promised to those who love him.

JAMES 1:12

Let's not get tired of doing what is good. At just the right time we will reap a harvest of blessing if we don't give up.

GALATIANS 6:9

Search for the LORD and for his strength;
  continually seek him.

1 CHRONICLES 16:11

Because of the joy awaiting [Jesus], he endured the cross, disregarding its shame. Now he is seated in the place of honor beside God's throne. Think of all the hostility he endured from sinful people; then you won't become weary and give up.

HEBREWS 12:2-3

We can rejoice, too, when we run into problems
and trials, for we know that they help us develop
endurance. And endurance develops strength
of character, and character strengthens our
confident hope of salvation. And this hope will
not lead to disappointment. For we know how
dearly God loves us, because he has given us the
Holy Spirit to fill our hearts with his love.

ROMANS 5:3-5

When troubles of any kind come your way,
consider it an opportunity for great joy. For
you know that when your faith is tested, your
endurance has a chance to grow. So let it grow,
for when your endurance is fully developed, you
will be perfect and complete, needing nothing.

JAMES 1:2-4

Let all that I am wait quietly before God,
   for my hope is in him.

PSALM 62:5

Dear brothers and sisters, never get tired of
doing good.

2 THESSALONIANS 3:13

Patient endurance is what you need now, so that you will continue to do God's will. Then you will receive all that he has promised.

HEBREWS 10:36

Unless the LORD builds a house,
    the work of the builders is wasted.
Unless the LORD protects a city,
    guarding it with sentries will do no good.
It is useless for you to work so hard
    from early morning until late at night,
anxiously working for food to eat;
    for God gives rest to his loved ones.

PSALM 127:1-2

Truly my soul finds rest in God;
    my salvation comes from him.

PSALM 62:1, NIV

Forgetting the past and looking forward to what lies ahead, I press on to reach the end of the race and receive the heavenly prize for which God, through Christ Jesus, is calling us.

PHILIPPIANS 3:13-14

YOU NEED HOPE

Rejoice in our confident hope. Be patient in trouble, and keep on praying.

ROMANS 12:12

I pray that God, the source of hope, will fill you completely with joy and peace because you trust in him. Then you will overflow with confident hope through the power of the Holy Spirit.

ROMANS 15:13

"I know the plans I have for you," says the LORD. "They are plans for good and not for disaster, to give you a future and a hope."

JEREMIAH 29:11

We are pressed on every side by troubles, but we are not crushed. We are perplexed, but not driven to despair. We are hunted down, but never abandoned by God. We get knocked down, but we are not destroyed.

2 CORINTHIANS 4:8-9

O Lord, you alone are my hope.
  I've trusted you, O LORD, from childhood.

PSALM 71:5

Be strong and courageous,
  all you who put your hope in the LORD!

PSALM 31:24

Because of our faith, Christ has brought us into
this place of undeserved privilege where we now
stand, and we confidently and joyfully look
forward to sharing God's glory.

ROMANS 5:2

Blessed are those who trust in the LORD
  and have made the LORD their hope and
    confidence.

JEREMIAH 17:7

I will keep on hoping for your help;
  I will praise you more and more.

PSALM 71:14

This same God who takes care of me will
supply all your needs from his glorious riches,
which have been given to us in Christ Jesus.

PHILIPPIANS 4:19

"My grace is all you need. My power works best
in weakness." So now I am glad to boast about
my weaknesses, so that the power of Christ can
work through me.

2 CORINTHIANS 12:9

I tell you the truth, those who listen to my
message and believe in God who sent me have
eternal life.

JOHN 5:24

YOU ARE IMPATIENT

Wait patiently for the LORD.
    Be brave and courageous.
    Yes, wait patiently for the LORD.

PSALM 27:14

Be patient in trouble, and keep on praying.

ROMANS 12:12

If we look forward to something we don't yet
have, we must wait patiently and confidently.

ROMANS 8:25

Let's not get tired of doing what is good. At just
the right time we will reap a harvest of blessing
if we don't give up.

GALATIANS 6:9

Be still in the presence of the LORD,
    and wait patiently for him to act.

PSALM 37:7

Control your temper,
  for anger labels you a fool.

ECCLESIASTES 7:9

Always be humble and gentle. Be patient with each other, making allowance for each other's faults because of your love.

EPHESIANS 4:2

Love is patient and kind. Love is not jealous or boastful or proud.

I CORINTHIANS 13:4

You must all be quick to listen, slow to speak, and slow to get angry.

JAMES 1:19

I am counting on the LORD;
  yes, I am counting on him.
  I have put my hope in his word.

PSALM 130:5

He will give eternal life to those who keep on doing good, seeking after the glory and honor and immortality that God offers.

ROMANS 2:7

Consider the farmers who patiently wait for the rains in the fall and in the spring. They eagerly look for the valuable harvest to ripen. You, too, must be patient. Take courage, for the coming of the Lord is near.

JAMES 5:7-8

The Twelve Verses to Remember When . . .

YOU ARE UNSURE OF YOURSELF

God saved you by his grace when you believed. And you can't take credit for this; it is a gift from God. Salvation is not a reward for the good things we have done, so none of us can boast about it.

EPHESIANS 2:8-9

Trust in the LORD with all your heart;
　　do not depend on your own understanding.
Seek his will in all you do,
　　and he will show you which path to take.

PROVERBS 3:5-6

I am certain that God, who began the good work within you, will continue his work until it is finally finished on the day when Christ Jesus returns.

PHILIPPIANS 1:6

You can pray for anything, and if you have faith, you will receive it.

MATTHEW 21:22

We live by believing and not by seeing.

2 CORINTHIANS 5:7

Faith comes from hearing, that is, hearing the Good News about Christ.

ROMANS 10:17

The LORD said to Samuel, "Don't judge by his appearance or height, for I have rejected him. The LORD doesn't see things the way you see them. People judge by outward appearance, but the LORD looks at the heart."

1 SAMUEL 16:7

[Jesus said,] "I tell you the truth, if you had faith even as small as a mustard seed, you could say to this mountain, 'Move from here to there,' and it would move. Nothing would be impossible."

MATTHEW 17:20

We were given this hope when we were saved.
(If we already have something, we don't need
to hope for it. But if we look forward to
something we don't yet have, we must wait
patiently and confidently.)

ROMANS 8:24-25

I tell you the truth, those who listen to my
message and believe in God who sent me have
eternal life. They will never be condemned for
their sins, but they have already passed from
death into life.

JOHN 5:24

See, God has come to save me.
    I will trust in him and not be afraid.
The LORD GOD is my strength and my song;
    he has given me victory.

ISAIAH 12:2

If you openly declare that Jesus is Lord and
believe in your heart that God raised him from
the dead, you will be saved.

ROMANS 10:9

YOU NEED COMFORT

All praise to God, the Father of our Lord Jesus Christ. God is our merciful Father and the source of all comfort. He comforts us in all our troubles so that we can comfort others. When they are troubled, we will be able to give them the same comfort God has given us.

2 CORINTHIANS 1:3-4

Sing for joy, O heavens!
    Rejoice, O earth!
    Burst into song, O mountains!
For the LORD has comforted his people
    and will have compassion on them in their
        suffering.

ISAIAH 49:13

God blesses those who are poor and realize their
        need for him,
    for the Kingdom of Heaven is theirs.
God blesses those who mourn,
    for they will be comforted.

God blesses those who are humble,
    for they will inherit the whole earth.

MATTHEW 5:3-5

Even when I walk
    through the darkest valley,
I will not be afraid,
    for you are close beside me.
Your rod and your staff
    protect and comfort me.

PSALM 23:4

Let your unfailing love comfort me,
    just as you promised me, your servant.

PSALM 119:76

The Holy Spirit helps us in our weakness. For
example, we don't know what God wants us to
pray for. But the Holy Spirit prays for us with
groanings that cannot be expressed in words.

ROMANS 8:26

He gives prosperity to the poor
    and protects those who suffer.

JOB 5:11

In that day you will sing:
  "I will praise you, O LORD!
You were angry with me, but not any more.
  Now you comfort me."

ISAIAH 12:1

Surely your goodness and unfailing love will
    pursue me
  all the days of my life,
and I will live in the house of the LORD
  forever.

PSALM 23:6

He heals the brokenhearted
  and bandages their wounds.

PSALM 147:3

After you have suffered a little while, he will
restore, support, and strengthen you, and he
will place you on a firm foundation.

1 PETER 5:10

You have sorrow now, but I will see you again; then
you will rejoice, and no one can rob you of that joy.

JOHN 16:22

PART 3

THE TWELVE VERSES EVERY CHRISTIAN SHOULD KNOW

*Heaven and earth will pass away, but
my words will never pass away.*

MATTHEW 24:35, NIV

This is how God loved the world:
He gave his one and only Son,
so that everyone who believes
in him will not perish but have
eternal life.

JOHN 3:16

I am the way, the truth, and the life. No one can come to the Father except through me.

JOHN 14:6

"I know the plans I have for you," says the LORD. "They are plans for good and not for disaster, to give you a future and a hope."

JEREMIAH 29:11

Love is patient and kind. Love is not jealous or boastful or proud or rude. It does not demand its own way. It is not irritable, and it keeps no record of being wronged. It does not rejoice about injustice but rejoices whenever the truth wins out. Love never gives up, never loses faith, is always hopeful, and endures through every circumstance.

I CORINTHIANS 13:4-7

I can do everything through Christ, who gives me strength.

PHILIPPIANS 4:13

Trust in the LORD with all your heart; do not depend on your own understanding. Seek his will in all you do, and he will show you which path to take.

PROVERBS 3:5-6

Faith shows the reality of what we hope for; it is the evidence of things we cannot see.

HEBREWS 11:1

Those who trust in the LORD will find new strength. They will soar high on wings like eagles. They will run and not grow weary. They will walk and not faint.

ISAIAH 40:31

Don't worry about anything;
instead, pray about everything.
Tell God what you need, and
thank him for all he has done.

PHILIPPIANS 4:6

Anyone who belongs to Christ
has become a new person.
The old life is gone; a new life
has begun!

2 CORINTHIANS 5:17

*We know that God causes
everything to work together
for the good of those who love
God and are called according
to his purpose for them.*

God saved you by his grace
when you believed. And you
can't take credit for this;
it is a gift from God.

EPHESIANS 2:8

Tips for Memorizing Scripture

Even though research shows that mental exercises like Scripture memorization decrease stress, increase brain capacity, and improve memory function, many people shy away from them. Committing dozens, if not hundreds, of Bible verses to memory seems too hard.

Happily, there are many tricks and tips available to help eliminate the fear factor and make memorization both easier and more enjoyable!

If you're new to Scripture memorization, or your memory simply isn't what it used to be, don't be discouraged. Remember, your brain is like a muscle. Working and stretching it will help make it stronger. And the more you practice, the sharper your memory is going to become. So don't be intimidated. Start small, stay focused, and repeat after me: "I can do everything through Christ, who gives me strength" (Philippians 4:13).

10 TIPS FOR MEMORIZING SCRIPTURE

1. Start with verses you are already familiar with.
2. Break longer verses into smaller chunks.
3. Say the verses aloud.
4. Write verses out multiple times in longhand. (For an extra memory boost, use your nondominant hand.)
5. Choose verses that are personal to you.
6. Create flash cards. Write the book, chapter, and verse on one side and the Scripture passage on the other. Make sure you practice them both ways.
7. Set the Scripture passage to music.
8. Practice with a friend. Remember, socialization is one of the twelve spiritual disciplines for improving your memory.
9. Write verses on Post-it notes and stick them up in your house, in your car, and at work so you can be reminded of them wherever you go.
10. Work verses into your daily prayer or meditation time, and ask God for his help in committing them to memory.

Healthy Snacks for Boosting Your Memory

In addition to Scripture meditation and memorization, one of the best things you can do to improve your memory is to eat right.* Remember, your brain uses 20 to 30 percent of the calories you consume and operates at its best when you're taking in healthy foods. If you regularly eat junk food, both your body and your mind suffer. To keep your memory strong, it is important to focus on eating brain-healthy food.

After committing to a nutritious diet, you will quickly notice that you have more energy and fewer cravings. Your focus, memory, and moods will also improve—and you may even have a flatter stomach.

The next time you're hungry, instead of reaching for the cookie jar, try grabbing one of these healthy snacks instead.

- Pistachios
- Carrots
- Walnuts
- Spinach
- Almonds
- Kale
- Cashews
- Asparagus
- Hazelnuts
- Cauliflower
- Pumpkin seeds
- Broccoli
- Sunflower seeds
- Bell peppers
- Sesame seeds
- Celery
- Chia seeds
- Swiss chard
- Flaxseeds
- Cabbage
- Watermelon
- Lentils
- Bananas
- Garbanzo beans
- Blueberries
- Avocados
- Cranberries
- Sweet potatoes
- Raspberries
- Quinoa
- Blackberries
- Black beans
- Apples
- Brussels sprouts
- Cherries
- Tomatoes
- Cantaloupe
- Green beans
- Red grapes
- Summer squash

*For information on many more ways to improve your memory and overall health, read my book *Memory Rescue*.

Easy Exercises to Help Improve Your Memory

Much like the muscles in your body, the parts of your brain that you activate and use regularly will strengthen, while the parts of your brain that you do not use will atrophy. That's why mental exercise is every bit as important as physical exercise for keeping both your body and your brain strong.

The best mental exercises involve acquiring new knowledge and doing things you haven't done before—like Scripture memorization. Whenever the brain does something over and over, it learns how to do it using less and less energy.

If you want to give your brain a good workout, try one of these simple yet effective exercises:

- Play language games like Scrabble, Boggle, and Scattergories, or work crossword puzzles and word-search puzzles.
- Play strategy games like chess, backgammon, dominoes, bridge, or mahjong.

- Play math games like sudoku or KenKen.
- Memorize poetry, Scripture passages, and famous historical dates.
- Set aside fifteen minutes in your day to learn something new.
- Take a class (a foreign language, cooking, or art course, for example). Challenge your brain to learn new things.
- Limit your screen time. Unless you're watching something educational, TV is usually a "no-brain" activity. In fact, studies show that adults who watch two or more hours of TV a day have a significantly higher risk of Alzheimer's disease than those who don't.
- Try using your nondominant hand to write, eat, or brush your teeth.
- Expose your brain to new experiences, scents, sights, and people by traveling somewhere you've never been before.
- Hang around with smart, interesting people who challenge your ideas and way of thinking.
- Listen to classical music, which research suggests can actually lower your blood pressure and improve your memory and cognitive function.

About the Author

Dr. Daniel G. Amen is a physician, a double board–certified psychiatrist, founder of Amen Clinics, a 10-time *New York Times* bestselling author, and an international speaker. Together with Pastor Rick Warren and Mark Hyman, MD, Dr. Amen is also one of the chief architects of Saddleback Church's Daniel Plan, a program to get the world healthy through religious organizations.

Dr. Amen has written, produced, and hosted many popular public television shows about the brain that have aired across North America. He has spoken for the National Security Agency, and his work has been featured in outlets including *Newsweek*, *Time* magazine, the *Huffington Post*, the *New York Times*, the *Washington Post*, the *Los Angeles Times*, and *Men's Health*.